MACHINES MADE SIMPLE

Inclined Planes

Written by Kirsty Holmes

KidHaven PUBLISHING

Published in 2026 by
KidHaven Publishing, an Imprint of
Greenhaven Publishing, LLC
2544 Clinton St., Buffalo, NY 14224

Written by: Kirsty Holmes
Edited by: Elise Carraway
Designed by: Amelia Harris

Cataloging-in-Publication Data
Names: Holmes, Kirsty.
Title: Inclined planes / Kirsty Holmes.
Description: Buffalo, NY : KidHaven Publishing, 2026. | Series: Machines made simple | Includes glossary and index.
Identifiers: ISBN 9781534550698 (pbk.) | ISBN 9781534550704 (library bound) | ISBN 9781534550711 (ebook)
Subjects: LCSH: Inclined planes--Juvenile literature. | Simple machines--Juvenile literature.
Classification: LCC TJ147.H65 2026 | DDC 621.8--dc23

Manufactured in the United States of America

CPSIA compliance information: Batch #CSKH26
For further information contact Greenhaven Publishing LLC
at 1-844-317-7404.

Please visit our website,
www.greenhavenpublishing.com.
For a free color catalog of all our high-quality books, call toll free 1-844-317-7404
or fax 1-844-317-7405.

Image Credits
Images courtesy of Shutterstock.com, unless otherwise stated. Cover – SeventyFour, JU.STOCKER, Artiste2d3d, HappyPictures. Recurring images – Onica Alexandru Sergiu. 2–3 – FamVeld, P24_Design, Heavypong. 4–5 – Digital Genetics, Matveev Aleksandr, Kittibowornphatnon. 6–7 – New Africa, Yuliya D'yakova, ViDI Studio, Ljupco Smokovski. 8–9 – Beekeepx, 24K-Production. 10–11 – lemono. 12–13 – Anadolu_Dizgi. 14–15 – ivi.photo93, CandyRetriever, Tanita_St. 16–17 – Dmytro Falkowskyi, AnnGaysorn, Blazic - guy. 18–19 – kornnphoto, FamVeld. 20–21 – acsen, SofiaV. 22–23 – Ljupco Smokovski, Ruslan Shevchenko, Lisavo, Richard Whitcombe.

Contents

WORDS THAT LOOK LIKE THIS CAN BE FOUND IN THE GLOSSARY ON PAGE 24.

Marvelous Machinery

Can you imagine what your life would be like without any machines? Machines help humans do all sorts of jobs. Life would be much more difficult without them!

WHAT JOBS DO MACHINES DO IN YOUR HOME?

Complicated machines do complicated jobs. They might have lots of parts. Simple machines do simple jobs and might have only one part. Both simple ramps and complicated factory equipment are types of machines.

WHAT DO YOU THINK THESE MACHINES DO?

What Is a Machine?

A machine is something that we use to do a job. Machines can help us do things we could not do on our own. Machines can also make tasks easier for us. Machines can do lots of different jobs.

Simple machines use forces to do different jobs. A force, such as a push or a pull, changes the speed or direction of an object.

What Is an Inclined Plane?

An inclined plane is a complicated name for a very simple machine. A plane is a smooth, even surface, such as a plank of wood. An inclined plane means the surface is raised higher at one end.

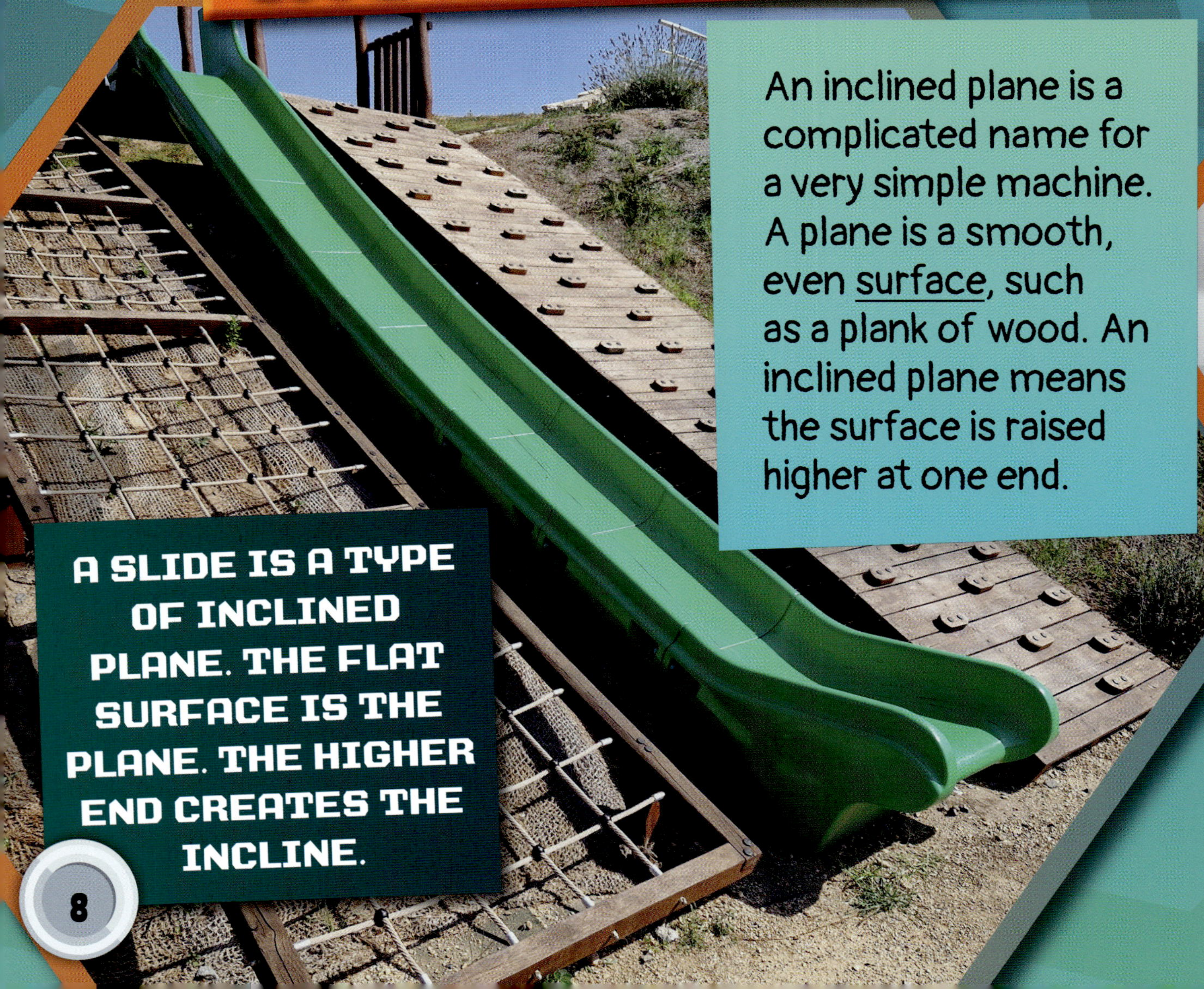

A SLIDE IS A TYPE OF INCLINED PLANE. THE FLAT SURFACE IS THE PLANE. THE HIGHER END CREATES THE INCLINE.

An inclined plane can also be called a ramp or a slope. We can use inclined planes to move loads up or down more easily than if we tried to move them ourselves.

INCLINED PLANES ARE VERY SIMPLE MACHINES WITH NO MOVING PARTS.

Parts of an Inclined Plane

The inclined plane has three main parts.

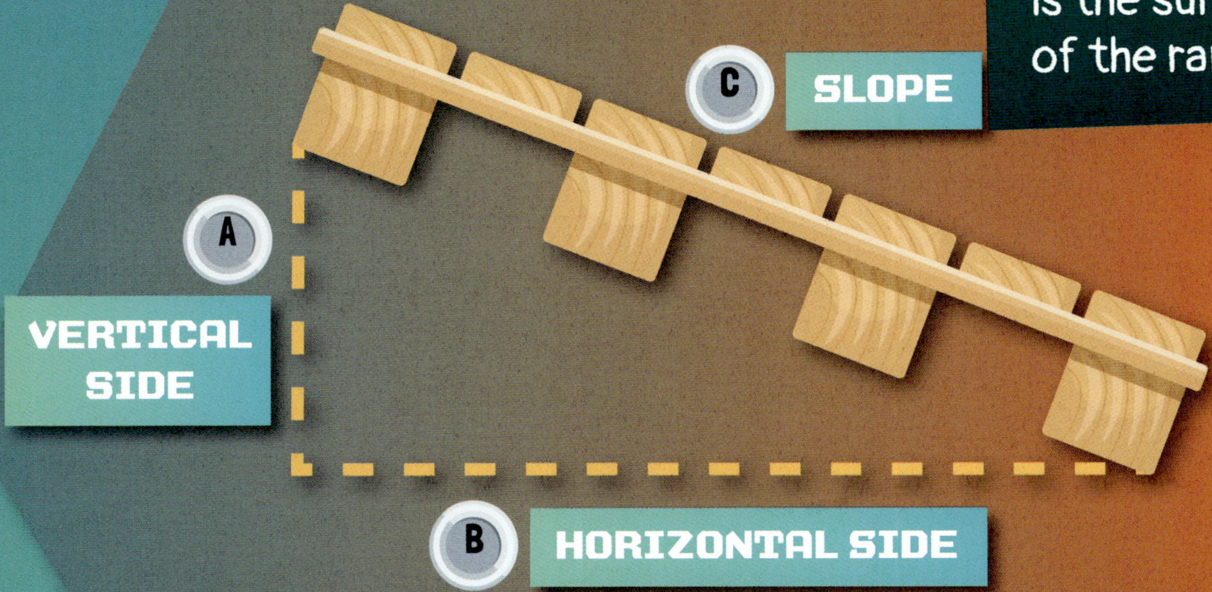

C: The slope is the surface of the ramp.

A: The vertical side is the distance from the top of the ramp in a straight line down to the ground.

B: The horizontal side is the distance from the bottom of the vertical side to the end of the slope.

A short vertical side and a long horizontal side gives a gentle slope. A long vertical side and a shorter horizontal side gives a steep slope.

WHERE HAVE YOU SEEN A GENTLE SLOPE? WHAT ABOUT A STEEP SLOPE?

Going Up

This worker is pushing a heavy box to the top of the ramp. He is using a push force to move it. This ramp has a steep slope because the horizontal side is quite short.

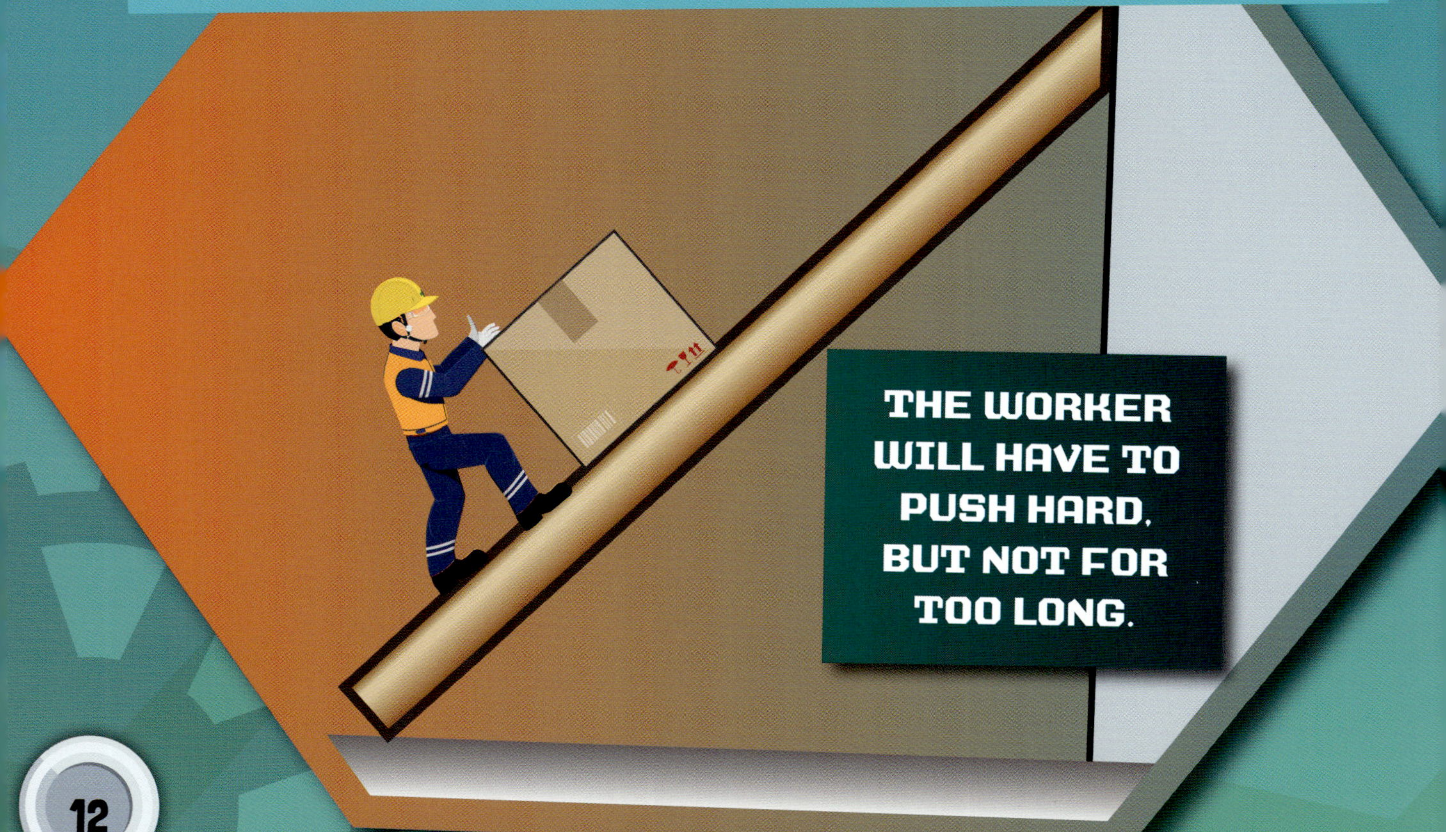

THE WORKER WILL HAVE TO PUSH HARD, BUT NOT FOR TOO LONG.

This ramp is a gentler slope. The horizontal side is longer. The worker will not have to use as much force to push the box to the top. However, they will have to push farther and for longer.

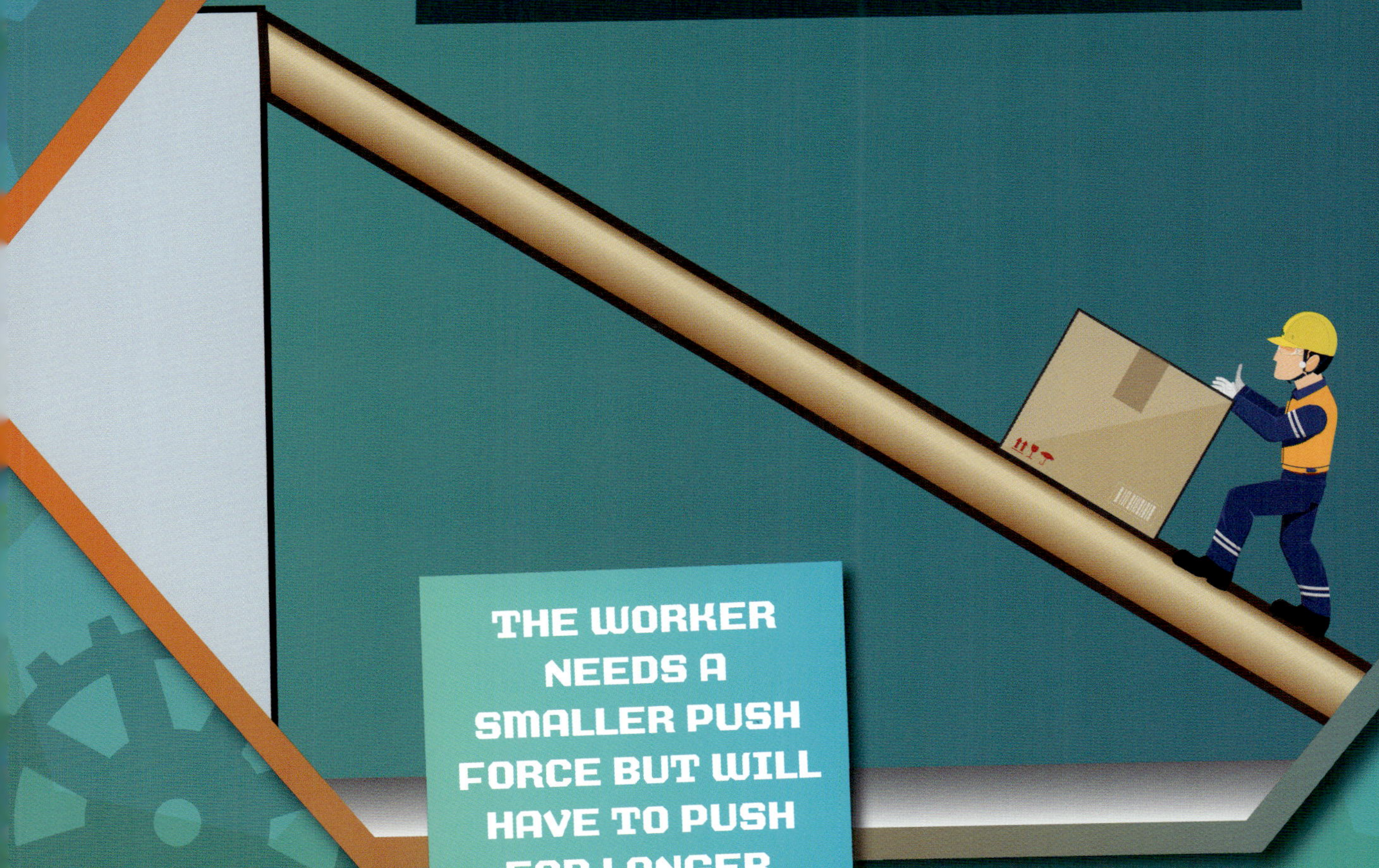

THE WORKER NEEDS A SMALLER PUSH FORCE BUT WILL HAVE TO PUSH FOR LONGER.

Going Down

An object at the top of an inclined plane will usually slide or roll downwards. This is because of a force called gravity. Gravity is the force that pulls everything down towards Earth's center.

OBJECTS ROLL FASTER DOWN STEEP SLOPES AND SLOWER DOWN GENTLE SLOPES.

Friction is a force that happens when two things rub against each other and grip together. More friction slows things down. Less friction speeds things up.

ROUGH SURFACES HAVE MORE FRICTION.

SMOOTH SURFACES HAVE LESS FRICTION.

Really Useful Ramps

Simple ramps are useful for all sorts of situations. Ramps can help us get to high places and are often easier to use than stairs. They do not need electricity or moving parts.

Sloping roofs let rain and snow slide off easily.

Ramps make places accessible for wheelchair users and people with strollers.

This sign tells you how steep the slope of a road is. Sloping roads help us drive up mountains.

Really Fun Ramps

Ramps and slopes can be useful, but they can also be fun! Biking, skateboarding, and roller-skating all become much more interesting when there is an inclined plane in the game!

SKATE PARK RAMPS HELP YOU GO FARTHER AND FASTER.

Inclined planes can be found all over the park, at the fair, and even in the water! How many fun ramps and slopes can you find while out and about?

HAVE YOU EVER BEEN ON A WATER SLIDE?

Really Old Ramps

Inclined planes are one of the oldest machines humans have used throughout history. Ramps and slopes may even have been used to move the heavy stones used to build the Egyptian pyramids.

CAN YOU SEE HOW RAMPS MIGHT HAVE MOVED THE STONES UP THE PYRAMIDS?

Even the ancient Greeks used ramps. Wagons, carts, and animals can use ramps, so they were an important part of many buildings.

THIS RAMP IS FROM THE RUINS OF THE ANCIENT CITY OF TROY.

Super Simple

Inclined planes make lots of fun activities possible. All of these activities use a ramp or slope. Can you name them all?

A

B

C

A: Sledding, B: Rollerblading, C: Skiing

Ramps can even save lives. First responders use ramps to launch boats into the sea quickly. They slide down the ramp to the rescue in only a few minutes. This type of ramp is called a slipway.

RAMPS ARE ALWAYS READY TO GO.

Glossary

accessible	available or able to be used by everyone
electricity	a kind of energy that is used for light and heat, and to power things
equipment	something made for a particular use, such as for jobs or sports
horizontal	flat or side-to-side; in line with the surface of the Earth
launch	to get something moving, such as by pushing a boat into water
loads	amounts of things to be carried or moved
ruins	old, broken-down buildings and structures
surface	the part of a thing that is flat, such as a tabletop or a wall
vertical	straight up-and-down; standing tall from the surface of the Earth

Index